Daddy's Girl

A Daughter's Walk With Her Abba Yahuah

Latisha Hanger

Disclaimer: This book is a work of nonfiction. However, certain names have been changed to protect the privacy of individuals. Any resemblance to actual persons, living or dead, or actual events is purely coincidental unless explicitly stated otherwise. The author has taken care to present events and conversations as truthfully and accurately as possible from their perspective. Where dialogue or scenarios have been recreated, they are based on the author's best recollection and are not intended to harm or misrepresent any individual. All views expressed are those of the author and do not reflect those of any organization, employer, or group.

ZOË Life
COACHING • CONSULTING • PUBLISHING

Table of Contents

Prologue:

Daddy's Girl is a heartfelt healing journey of a daughter's walk with her true father, Abba Yahuah.

This book invites you to take this journey with a woman named Abigail. This journey details parts of Abigail's life and how through each experience, her Abba Yahuah was there holding her hand, strengthening her, restoring her, and most of all, loving her.

Abigail's journey will elaborate on how the Most High Yahuah taught her to extract the fatherly lessons out of each experience. Abigail was not only delivered from the hands of the enemy, but she was also delivered from her self-inflicting torment.

Daddy's Girl is more than a story, it's a call to come home, to reconnect with your divine identity, to find healing from rejection and any father wounds, to embrace the tender guiding voice of your Abba Yahuah, and to walk boldly in daughterhood and spiritual royalty.

With love,

Latisha

Part 1:

Unequally Yoked

Abigail met Gabriel through her supervisor from work. One Friday before leaving the office, Abigail's supervisor asked her, "*Hey Abby, what you doing this weekend? I'm having a graduation party for my daughter, and I would love for you to come.*"

Abigail replied, "*Certainly. I would love to come party with you guys this weekend. What's your address and what time should I be there?*"

The following morning, Abigail conducted her normal routine. Then around 5 p.m., she got a ride to her supervisor's house to join in the festivities. Once Abigail arrived at her supervisor's house she greeted everyone that she knew and was introduced to those that she didn't. With the greetings and introductions out of the way, Abby began to do what most party goers do, *turn up*. Once the party started to wind down, Abby's supervisor asked her to sleep over. Abby complied.

The next morning, while at the dining room table discussing the previous night's events/shenanigans, there was a knock at the door. There entered Gabriel, her supervisor's little brother.

℘

Now, Abigail was very pleasing to the eye. Beautiful face, nice body, and a beautiful spirit. Gabriel ("Gabe" for short) was introduced to Abby, and he looked at her as if she was a whole snack. Abby then excused herself from the table and went into the restroom. When she came back out, she invited Gabe out onto the balcony to smoke a blunt with her. He was in awe. Gabe, right then and there, had determined that Abby was the perfect woman for him.

At that time in Abby's life, she was not looking to be in a relationship with anyone. She had considered Gabriel just a really cool homeboy, but Abby knew Gabe wanted more. She wasn't ready to give that just yet. For the next few weeks, Gabe and Abby were inseparable. Months had passed and Abby realized she was still at her supervisor's house, only going home to grab clothes and a few items.

℘

Summer holidays rolled around and Abby's favorite person in the whole wide world came into town for a visit, her grandmother. There was no way Abby was going to miss out on spending time with her. Abigail rose early one morning, packed up all of her belongings she had brought over to her supervisor's house, woke Gabe, told him she was headed home, and asked him to lock the door behind her.

Two weeks went by and Gabriel had heard no word from Abigail, for she was enjoying her time spent with her grandmother. By the third week, Abigail began to miss Gabriel's presence. They had not exchanged numbers, so Abigail called her supervisor's home phone.

"*Hey, Jade. How have you guys been?*"

"*Hey, stranger. We've been well. How about you?*"

"That's good. I've been good. I've been entertaining my grandmother for the last few weeks while she's here on vacation. I was calling to see if I could speak to Gabe. Is he around?"

"Yeah, sure, hold on."

Gabe thought the day he got up and locked the door, that Abby had walked out of his life and that he would never see her again.

Gabe and Abby set up a time and place to meet up, for they had discovered that they both were missing each other.

Gabriel let Abigail know that he wanted to be in her life and that he wanted to be more than just a homeboy. From there, Gabriel and Abigail began to date. On their fourth date, Abigail invited Gabriel to her apartment to stay with her that night, where they consummated the relationship.

That night, Gabriel asked Abigail to be his wife.

Gabriel moved his things into Abigail's apartment the next day.

Now, just a little background on Abigail. She was raised in the church by her grandmother. She was an avid student of the Bible. She sang in the church choir, and any and every event that was taking place at the church, she was present. Abigail began to miss her church life, so she began to ask Gabriel of his beliefs and relationship with the Most High Yahuah. which was out of order. Gabe told Abby that his family was Catholic and that he did not attend church with them, nor did he believe in the Bible because it was written by a man. For some reason, Abigail saw that statement as an opportunity, a teachable moment. Abigail should have regarded Gabriel's response for exactly what it was, a great big old red flag, and she should have ran for the hills. Abigail and Gabriel had been shacked up for about a month when he came home and told Abigail that he had gotten fired from his job. When Abby inquired as to what happened, Gabe began to tell her how he had cursed out his boss and was fired for insubordination. Abby thought,

"*Wow*", because she had never heard nor seen anyone behave in such a manner toward an authority figure. Abby was now having to downsize from a two-bedroom apartment to a one-bedroom since she was now paying for two people to survive. A few months later, no job in sight from Gabe, they were moving out of their apartment and in with Gabe's sister, Abby's supervisor. Due to Abby's circumstances, she allowed a spirit of depression to come up on her, and it was hard for her to even get out of bed on some days. Abby was fired from her job due to her attendance. With Gabe and Abby out of work, Jade was ready for them to leave her home. And so, they did. Gabe and Abby began to live in their car. Gabe reached out to his mother for some help, and she sent him to work for his stepfather. While working there, Gabe made a few dollars, enough to get them a hotel room for a few nights. They would sleep in a hotel for a few nights, and they would sleep in their car for a few nights.

One morning, Abby woke up feeling sick and could no longer stand the smell of smoke, cigarettes, nor marijuana. So, she suggested that Gabe pick up a pregnancy test. Regardless of their circumstances, that plus sign on that test result brought them much joy and happiness. Abby knew in her heart that she could not endure a pregnancy living the way that they were living, between hotels and their car, so Abby said to Gabe, "*I want to go home to my grandmother.*"

Gabe said he would first ask his stepfather if he would increase his pay so that they could stay and get their own apartment again. Abby agreed to wait for Gabe's stepfather's response to his request. Gabe came back to the hotel very late and very intoxicated. Not only did his stepfather not agree to a pay raise, but he also fired Gabe for even asking. The plan was to head home for Abby to have a peaceful pregnancy. There was one thing Gabe wanted to do before they headed out of state.

Gabe had determined in his mind that his stepfather was going to pay for his decision to terminate him. Gabe broke into his stepfather's shop, his place of business, and robbed him of every tool necessary for the work that he did. Gabe went all around town to about five different pawn shops and pawned the stolen tools off. The next morning, they packed up the car with all their belongings gassed up and headed out of town with roughly $2,500 in their possession. The trip to Abby's home was about a three-hour drive. An hour and a half into the trip, Abby felt a cramp in her belly, and she felt very nauseous. She had just attributed it to the uncomfortably long ride.

Grandmother welcomed Gabe and Abby into her home with opened arms. She was so happy to see Abby (who she had raised). Once settled in this new town for Gabe, but home to Abby, Gabe found employment through a temp agency with work at a construction site. Things were already beginning to look promising for them.

One Saturday morning, Abby felt as though she had some serious pressure on her stomach. She went and sat on the toilet. Abby felt like something was not right in her stomach. She began to pour buckets of sweat from her forehead. Abby had been in the restroom for a long while, so Gabe came to look in on her.

When he saw her pale face and how wet she was with sweat, he said, "*I'm going to get Grandmother.*"

Abby said, "*No, I'm all right. Just give me a moment the feeling will pass.*"

Gabe then helped her off of the toilet and into the bed, where nothing had changed.

Gabe went and got grandmother, who said, "*Call an ambulance,*" as soon as she saw how pale and wet Abby looked. By now, Abby was drenched with sweat. It looked like someone had threw buckets of water on her. She was gasping for air. Once she made it to the emergency room, everything went black. Abby had passed out.

When Abigail had awakened in the recovery room, she couldn't even speak. She was discombobulated, not knowing how she had even gotten here. Sleep overtook her. Abby awakened again, this time she was in a private hospital room, with Gabriel asleep on a small bed right next to hers.

Abigail looked at Gabriel and inquired," *What happened?*"

Gabriel replied, *"We lost the baby.*"

Abigail wept. A few moments later, the doctor came in and explained to Abigail that the pregnancy was in her fallopian tube. What happened while Abigail was on the toilet was that the tube ruptured and that her stomach began to fill up with blood. The reason she was gasping for breath was that the blood began to touch her liver and she was dying. They were able to remove the fetus, and while sucking out the blood from the rupture, simultaneously they were transfusing blood back into her. Abigail was advised that 50% of the blood in her whole body was in her stomach, and that she had to have six pints of blood transfused back into her body. Abigail was in the hospital for about three days, and on the fourth day, she was ready to be released, but the doctor wanted to test the hemoglobin levels in her blood before releasing her. Two phlebotomists came in and tried to find a vein to draw blood with no success. Abigail was convinced that the third one was sent by her Abba Yahuah. He was soft-spoken, very kind, and gentle with her. A vein was found almost immediately. Her levels were tested and needless to say, Abby had to have one more pint of blood transfused and was released from the hospital two days later.

In the months to come, while Abby was healing, the relationship between her and Gabe became very volatile. Neither of them were emotionally intelligent enough to express how they were truly feeling about the loss that they had just suffered. Gabe couldn't hold down a job. They had progressed from constantly arguing to fist-fighting one another. Abigail was tired of the strain and discomfort she felt she was putting on Grandmother, so they had decided to go back to Gabe's home state to try it again. Grandmother had beseeched Abigail to let Gabriel go back on his own, but Abby had Gabe in her ear begging her to not leave him. Abby had devised a plan to stay with her aunt who had moved to Gabe's home state. Abigail called her aunt, and she asked if she and Gabriel could stay with her until they got on their feet. Once they returned back to Gabe's home state, about two weeks in, Abigail went back to work. Gabriel was only able to get day work from time to time, no solid gigs were opening any doors to him.

Abigail began to think that the attack on their relationship was because they had not legally tied the knot. So, Abby went and bought them some wedding bands from a nearby pawn shop, paid for a little ceremony at a chapel, paid for the marriage license, and a week later she and Gabe were husband and wife.

Soon, Gabriel and Abigail were finally living in their own apartment again. Abby tried to incorporate Bible studies in their weekly routine, and they even began to go to church service on Sundays. Wouldn't you know, that solved nothing. The fighting got worse.

One day, Abby had convinced Gabe to get baptized thinking that it might help their spiritual battle. Boy, was that an affront to the enemy, 'cause all hell broke loose. Gabriel began drinking heavily and drugs (other than marijuana) were in heavy rotation for him as well. Gabe began robbing stores, people, and he even would take money from Abby's purse from time to time. Abigail could take no more. She confronted Gabriel about his misdeeds. Abby was unaware that this conversation was going to initiate the fight of her life. Gabriel was enraged. He hit Abigail so hard she could have sworn she saw stars. The fight was to be had all throughout the whole of the apartment.

Abigail was worn out and she yelled, "*ENOUGH*!"

Gabe stopped hitting her long enough for Abby to throw on her wig, grab her purse, put on some tennis shoes, and leave out the door. Abby had barely made it up the street when she heard Gabe calling her. She turned to look, and

Gabe was sprinting up the street toward her. Abby dropped her purse and squared up for another battle. They were fighting on the hood of a car that belonged to a neighbor that lived up the street from where they resided. When the neighbor heard all of the commotion, they came out of their house.

They could be heard saying, "*Stop hitting her like that!*"

Abby said, "*You better stop hitting me Gabe*."

Gabe threatened, "*Who's going to stop me*?"

Abby replied, "*Yahusha*," also known as Jesus Christ.

Gabriel froze right where he stood.

The neighbor intervened and said to Abby, "*Come in here honey.*" While Abby went inside the neighbor's house, Gabe stood there frozen.

Once Abigail got inside the neighbor's house, Gabe began trying to kick the neighbor's door down. He was trying to snatch the bars off their windows. He was adamant on getting to Abby. Before Gabe could get to her, the police had been called and arrived on the scene just in time to put Gabe in handcuffs and escort him to their vehicle. Abby was able to tell the officers what had transpired between her and Gabe. Gabe was then arrested and taken away to jail immediately. Back at the apartment, Abigail was planning on leaving. She called her grandmother, told her everything that had transpired between her and Gabe, and even sent her pictures of her face. Grandmother could visibly see Abby's eye was swelling shut. Gabe had done some serious damage this time.

Grandmother said to her granddaughter, "*Come home*."

Summary/Conclusion Part 1:

- Abigail should have asked Gabriel about his beliefs and relationship with The Most High Yahuah during their dating process, well before she had sexual intercourse with him.
- Abigail was gifted with the knowledge and understanding on how to teach which is why she perceived Gabriel's statement about church and the Bible as a teachable moment.
- Abigail and Gabriel were **Unequally Yoked**. Things began to go in a downward spiral because Abigail had aligned herself with an unrighteous man of the world.
- Grandmother was one of the Guardian Angels Yahuah had placed in Abigail's life.

Part 2:

Everything Happens For A Reason

Abigail arrived home to find that grandmother was now attending a new worship assembly. Grandmother introduced Abigail to a beautiful young lady that was a member of the church named Simone. Upon getting to know one another, Abby and Simone discovered that they had a lot in common. Both Abby and Simone had married men that had mental issues, and both men were abusive. Abigail and Simone were also in the process of divorcing these men. Abigail and Simone hit it off from the gate, and a beautiful sisterhood was initiated. After every service on Sunday, Abigail would go over to Simone's house for fellowship and Sunday dinner. Abigail began to feel as though this bond was the inception of her healing process. A few months into this newly cemented friendship/ sistership, Simone asked Abby if she would not only house-sit for her, but also watch over her most precious gift, her 15-year-old son named Andrew. Abigail was honored that

Simone trusted her and said yes! So, Simone packed up and went on a seven-day cruise.

Abigail and Andrew had an auntie-nephew relationship with one another and were super excited to spend this time with each other. Abigail would go to work in the morning, and Andrew would go to school. Once their work and school day was completed, they would come home, watch TV shows together, cook together, or sometimes just have a good old conversation about how their day went. Simone would call and check in with them once daily, just to make sure all was well. On day 6 of Simone's trip, she reached out to Abigail to let her in on what had taken place while she was on her cruise. Simone had reconciled with her husband Eric. Simone advised Abigail that when she returned home from her trip, that her husband Eric would be accompanying her. Abigail did not feel right about Simone's decision, which she never voiced out loud to her sister. Instead, all Abby said was, "*Sis, if you truly believe that this is what's best, may the Most High Yahuah, bless your union.*" Once Simone returned home, Abby went home to Grandmother's with a bit of sadness in her heart.

℘

Abby and Simone didn't talk on the phone as frequently as they had prior to her and her husband returning home. Although Abigail and Simone didn't talk as much on the phone, after service on Sunday, Abby still went home with Simone and her family for fellowship and Sunday dinner. That hadn't changed. Abby, Simone, Eric, and Andrew began hanging out together. Restaurants, concerts, barbecues, birthday parties, they even had new movie Fridays on their calendar. It was during this time that Abigail had decided to enroll in college to obtain a degree in Business. Simone had also learned that she was pregnant and asked Abigail to be the godmother of her expecting baby. Abigail loved children. She was extremely honored and accepted Simone and Eric's requisition. Since Abigail had been spending so much time with Simone and her family, she was asked if she would like to live with them. Abby accepted. She was focusing on school and how she would be a great help to Simone once the baby arrived.

℘

A few months of classes and a few months into living with Simone and her family, Abby was notified by Grandmother that the doctors had discovered cancerous cells behind Grandmother's stomach, known as pancreatic cancer. Grandmother was almost instantly scheduled to have surgery to remove the cancerous tissues. Grandmother was 76 years old, and cancer was a lot to be going through at this stage in her life. It seemed as though the surgery had gone well, and once Grandmother was released from the hospital, Abby, her aunts, and cousins all took shifts in the care/recovery of her. In the midst of all this, Simone had given birth to a beautiful, healthy baby girl. Abigail was now in between Grandmother's and Simone's house, all the while still attending her classes. Grandmother's doctor had scheduled her to endure chemotherapy at the ripe old age of 76 which caused her to be very Ill and weakened her tremendously. Abigail moved back in with Grandmother, visiting Simone and her family whenever she had some free time. On the days Abby would visit Simone, she could clearly see that Simone's countenance was different.

℘

Simone had informed Abigail that she was attending therapy due to postpartum depression. Abigail did what she thought was best, and that was to speak life into her sister. Abigail was constantly on the move between classes, Grandmother, Simone, and her family. She had no time to process anything, really. One day, Abigail reached out to Simone to confirm whether or not she would be at home so that she could grab a few of her books she had left at Simone's house. Abigail needed to study/review for an upcoming exam at school. Simone had advised Abigail that she was out of town and that Eric would be available for Abby to go and pick up the books she required. Abigail reached out to Eric to verify what time he would be home. Once an agreed-upon time was set, Abby went about her day. The following evening, Eric was notified by Abby that she was on her way to pick up her books. Once Abby reached Simone's house, the usual brotherly/sisterly greetings were concluded, and she went about retrieving what she had come for, her books. Eric noticed that Abigail was all done and headed towards the door to make her exit back to Grandmother's house. So, he asked the one question that he knew would stop her in her tracks.

"*How's everything going with grandmother?*" Abigail began to open up and start a whole conversation on grandmother's condition/state.

Eric made a statement on how he perceived the experience was affecting Abigail and offered her a drink, (something strong, not wine, juice, nor water) and to have a seat, take a breather. Abigail accepted both. Now seated, Abigail had taken a sip of what was in her glass, she hadn't even realized just how anxious she really was. Abby was anxious about Grandmother, school, Simone and even a little bit about the divorce she was going through with Gabriel. As Abby was speaking about grandmother's health/condition, she could hear Eric ask, "*Need a refill*?"

Abby heard herself say, "*Sure*." Eric then began to ask Abigail questions about her relationship with Gabriel and what had gone wrong. Once Abby was finished speaking of the details of her experience in life with Gabe, she noticed that the bottle they had been drinking from was totally desolate. At this point in Abby's life, the strongest drink that she would consume was wine. Abigail was intoxicated. Abigail thought she was trippin' when she heard Eric say, "*You know I'm feeling you, right?*" Abby proceeded to advise Eric that she viewed him as a brother and someone she would never be interested in, in no shape or form.

Abigail tried to get up and take her leave because of the direction the conversation had turned. But when her whole world began to spin, she asked Eric if it would be alright if she could just sleep it off on the sofa. Eric then recommended that she sleep it off in he and Simone's bed. Abby refused, "*No. Eric, I love your wife. She is my sister and my best friend. I would never do anything that would cause her pain.*"

Eric responded, *"I love my wife too, I just want you to lay with me."* Abby refused to grant Eric's request and began to feel sick. Abby went to the restroom and began to throw up all the contents in her stomach. Once her stomach was void of anything, Abby went and laid down on the sofa. Eric had approached the sofa where Abby lay, grabbed her by the arm, and began to pull her into their bedroom. Abby's head was spinning; her world was reeling. Once they reached the bed in the room, Abby passed out. This was more than Abby's mind could contemplate.

Abigail regained consciousness to find Eric removing her clothes. Abby was too afraid to fight, for she knew Eric had no problem hitting women, nor did she have enough control of her motor skills to do so. Despite this being the very thing Abby had said "NO" to, she was now laying back and allowing it to happen. Once Eric had gotten what he wanted, (not for Abby to just lay in the bed with him) he allowed Abigail to stumble her way back onto the sofa. Early the next morning, Abigail had awakened and prepared to leave when Eric came out of his bedroom and asked Abby, "*What are you going to tell Simone?*" Abby said, "*I'll tell her that I just came over to get my books.*" Abby left Simone's and arrived at Grandmother's house, where her cousin Connie was on duty. Abby almost vomited all over Connie. When Connie asked Abigail, was she all right, Abigail told Connie that Eric had taken what she did not offer freely. Abigail gave Connie every detail of the previous night's events. Connie advised Abigail to tell

Simone all that had taken place, and Abby had agreed that she would.

℘

Abigail truly desired to inform her sister Simone of what had happened with Eric, but what was at the forefront of Abigail's mind was that Simone had just had a brand new baby and that she also was seeing a therapist for postpartum depression. The last thing Abigail wanted was to cause her sister with a brand-new baby any added stress/pressure. Abigail decided to withhold her wretched experience that took place with Eric from Simone. From that point on, Abigail and Simone did nothing together. The only time they saw each other, or even spoke to one another, was Sundays at church. And even that would be brief. Simone had just equated Abby's behavior to be a reflection of what was going on with Grandmother. The heaviness of everything that was happening in Abby's life began to show up as stress that caused her to have allergic reaction type symptoms. Abby would break out into hives for no reason. Her lips, fingers, and eyes would swell up for no apparent reason. Abby's hands and feet would itch so bad, she would scratch or rub them until they were almost raw. Abby would take Benadryl, which helped nothing. Abby went to see an allergen specialist to advise her of what she was allergic to. When the test came back that Abby was not allergic to anything, Abby was advised by the specialist that stress can cause the symptoms that she had been experiencing. For the next two months, Abby had to take Allegra-D to combat the stress-induced allergic reactions. After Abby was told that Simone and her family had moved to another city, Abby was no longer subjected to seeing Eric's face on Sunday mornings. Interestingly enough, those allergic reactions went away almost immediately, permanently.

℘

Although Abby was relieved of some stress, Grandmother was not doing so well. Grandmother had to be admitted back to the hospital. Abigail and her family received the horrible news that Grandmother was not going to make it. For a couple of days in Grandmother's hospital room, there was praising and worshiping as the Most High Yahuah called Grandmother home to be with Him. Abigail was totally devastated, so much so that she reached out to Gabriel. A few months after Grandmother's passing, Abigail was back with Gabriel. Both with new jobs, in their own place, all appeared to be well with Gabe and Abby. They even were riding in a new truck. Three months in and what seemed to be a good decision of reconciliation, Gabe would go missing for two to three days at a time. Abby would call and text Gabe repeatedly. Then Abby decided to go look for him in the places she thought he would be. Abby was able to locate Gabe at one of his friends' houses. Once she found him, he would come home. The next time

Gabe went MIA, Abby first went to the spot where she located him the last time. Gabe was nowhere in sight, so Abby called Gabe again and again with no response. Abby said to herself, "*I'm going to call one more time.*" Gabe answered. When Abby questioned him of his whereabouts and who he was with, Gabe's response was, "*Isn't it obvious? I found somebody else. I don't want to be with you anymore. I want children, and you can't have children."*

Abigail felt as though her very breath was snatched from her. All she could think to do was hang up the phone. Abby was in total disbelief of what had just taken place, the words that were just spoken to her. She couldn't even cry. Abigail put on some praise music and began to seek Yahuah. Within a few hours, the Holy Spirit (Ruach Ha'qodesh) began to direct Abby's path. First, she thanked her Abba Yahuah for keeping her mind, (she definitely could have lost it) next, she texted Gabe, (seeing as she knew he wouldn't answer her calls) that if he did not bring the truck to her, she would report it as stolen to the police. Then she reached out to her aunt that lived in a state Gabe knew nothing about and was as far away from him as she could possibly get. Abigail began to pack all her belongings when she got a call from Gabe telling her where she could pick up the truck. Abby located the truck to find that Gabe had pulled out all the stereo system, every speaker, and tweeter that was installed. Gabe figured he had to deliver one last gut punch to Abby before they went their separate ways. Abigail located the truck, drove the truck home, loaded it up with her belongings, then hit the road to Annie's house.

Summary/Conclusion Part 2:

- Abigail desired to return from whence she came, Home. Grandmother was home for Abigail. In the presence of Yahuah is home. In the presence of Yahuah is peace and tranquility. In actuality what we all are seeking is to be in the presence of Yahuah, back from whence we came.
- Abigail and Simone met in a broken place (both of them). Abigail and Simone's sisterhood was not strong enough where Abigail could be honest with Simone about her reconciliation with Eric.
- Abigail's naivete led her to believe that people who were church members did not cause harm to one another. Abigail believed that it was acceptable to serve Yahuah and still do worldly deeds.
- Abigail viewed Eric as her brother in Christ/brother-in-law assuming that he had her best interest at heart and would not cause her any harm.

Abigail's reaction to that horrible experience alone with Eric is an indicator of when silence makes you sick/ill.

Part 3:

The Great Battle

A good cry, praise and worship, and an in-depth conversation with her Abba Yahuah, Abigail arrived at her aunt's house feeling motivated and renewed. Once Abigail got settled in, Abigail informed her aunt of the events that had taken place, the events with Gabriel and with Eric. They cried together, they prayed together, then they rejoiced together for the new things that the Most High Yahuah was about to do in Abby's life. With her truck now completely unloaded, Abby was moved into her aunt's house and for the next few days, Abigail was on a mission to find a new place of employment. A couple of months and Abby was hired on at a prominent company with great pay and excellent benefits. Now with all that had taken place with Gabe and Eric, Abby had no desire to date men, in fact she had sworn off men and during the times she was alone she had begun consuming lesbian pornography. To keep it all the way real, Abby was feeling a little lonely.

When the scriptures say that the enemy/Satan, walks about seeking whom he can devour, that is absolute facts.

℘

Abigail began training for her new position. Abby walked in with confidence that she would be focused on this company and move up with purpose, not allowing any man to smile up in her face and vice versa (being a distraction). Abby's mind was made up on her future. But then, guess who gravitated to her in her training class? A beautiful lesbian named Diana. Diana was a tool for the enemy. She was very beautiful, long flowing jet-black hair, highly intelligent, dressed dope, smelled amazing and very ambitious. During the day, Abigail and Diana got better acquainted, and during the night, Abigail was consistently consuming lesbian pornography. From what Abigail and Diana had learned of one another, they became intrigued. Abigail and Diana had exchanged phone numbers. Now they were talking during the day at work and talking on the phone at night after work. What drew Abigail to Diana was her vision to create, her passion, her drive, and how she had plans mapped out for her future.

℘

Days turned into weeks. Weeks turned into months. Abigail and Diana were getting seriously attached to one another at this point. One evening, after working some overtime, Diana asked Abby if she wanted to hang out. Abby accepted the invite. Abigail met up with Diana at a nearby restaurant where they had some tacos and watched a soccer match on the TV. Before the night was over, Diana asked Abigail if she could kiss her. Abigail agreed. After what seemed like a forever kiss, Diana invited Abigail back to her apartment. Abby accepted the invite. Night after night, Abigail had been watching on her phone women having sex with women. Once back at Diana's place, Abigail and Diana did in real life what she had been watching on her phone.

℘

Abigail and Diana were now in a relationship, practically living together. Abigail would spend the night at Diana's house almost every night. They would have sex on a regular basis. Abigail was actually in a full-blown lesbian relationship.

A few months into their relationship, Abigail and Diana decided to take a trip out of town. They got dressed up and went sightseeing. When the night was winding down, Abby and Diana went back to their hotel room, Abby got undressed, climbed into bed and was asleep almost immediately. Diana was not happy. The next morning, while they were preparing to head out for breakfast, Abigail could sense that Diana was feeling some type of way.

When Abby asked Diana what the issue was, Diana replied, *"I think that this relationship has run its course."*

Abigail asked, "*Is it because we didn't have sex last night?*"

Diana then replied, *"Absolutely."*

Abigail was a little taken aback by Diana's response. Abby and Diana had their first disagreement. Abby recognized that she felt different with Diana. She didn't feel anxious or enraged. They actually talked it out logically. There was no shouting, and it did not get physical. Abigail and Diana had come to an agreement to enjoy what was left of their vacation.

Once they arrived back home from their trip, Abigail broke it off with Diana. She just couldn't get over the fact that the sole motivating factor for Diana remaining in this relationship with her was sex. Abby perceived that being in a relationship with Diana was no different than being in a relationship with a man that only wanted her for sex.

Abigail and Diana would see each other at work every day and they kept it cordial, although at night Diana would blow up Abby's phone, beseeching her to reconcile. After a couple of weeks, Abby complied with Diana's pleas. Back together, Diana seemed different. Diana appeared to be enamored with Abby. Abigail and Diana appeared to be in a good place.

℘

A few months went by and all seemed to be well. Abby was on her way home from Diana's one morning and felt a cramp in her belly. Once she arrived home, the pain began to feel familiar. Abby drove herself to the emergency room where the pain began to grow more and more intense. So intense that while they were asking her intake questions, Abby fainted.

When Abby awakened, Diana was standing beside her bed. Diana called for the nurse. The nurse called for the doctor, and when the doctor came in, she advised Abby that there was a tumor on her uterus that had grown into the size of a foot, and the pain that she was feeling was, one by one, the veins that had formed around the tumor began to pop. The familiar feeling that Abigail felt was the same feeling she had when her fallopian tube ruptured from her tubal pregnancy a few years back. The doctor had advised Abby that the tumor was not cancerous, nor did she have cancer. But what was recommended was a total hysterectomy, which caused Abigail to think that she would never be able to have children. Abigail then reached out to her aunt, and let her know what had happened to her. They cried together. They prayed together. Then they rejoiced together for the new thing that The Most High Yahuah was about to do in Abby's life. Abigail decided to not go through with a total hysterectomy procedure. In the back of her mind, she still had the desires and maybe even the hopes of being a mother.

Abigail's release from the hospital was approaching, so Abby turned to Diana and asked if it would be okay if she recovered at home with her. Diana was in full agreement.

℘

They arrived at Diana's condo. Diana lived in a two-story where Abby had to climb all the way up the stairs to get to where she would be recovering, Diana's bedroom. Abby settled in.

Diana turned and told her, "*I'll be back, love. I'm going to go hang out with my cousin for a little while.*"

Abby felt some type of way. Due to the pain medication, Abby was in and out of sleep but noticed that Diana had not yet returned home. Abby most certainly felt some type of way at this. Upon her return home Diana awakened Abby with a full-blown meal for her to eat (which she could not). Abby then advised Diana that soups, sherbert, sorbet was all she could digest. For a total of three days, Abby stayed with Diana. Diana went to work in the morning and went out every night. Abigail could sense something was not right.

On the fourth morning when Diana left for work, Abigail quietly gathered her things, wrote Diana a breakup letter, left it on her dresser and drove herself home. Diana's calls lit up Abby's phone all day with no response. By evening,

Diana was at Abby's doorstep. They stood across from one another, tension thick in the air. They discussed what had transpired. Abigail's voice steady but heavy, she let Diana know how she felt she was misled to believe that Diana would be there for her when she needed her the most. Abigail was disappointed in Diana.

She voiced to Diana, "*I didn't need you to bathe or wipe me, I just needed you to bring me food whenever I got hungry and possibly grant me a little bit of conversation from time to time.*"

Abigail had assumed that since she was in a relationship with Diana, that meant Diana cared for her. Abby advised Diana that she had to basically take care of herself during her time of recovery.

Abby said to Diana "*What's the point of me being with someone if I have to take care of myself?*"

Diana swallowed, the truth landing hard, she understood that this time Abby was not willing to reconcile. Abby was not looking for a fix. They were going to go their separate ways for good. Abigail was done.

A few more days of recovery were needed before Abigail returned to work. In this time, Abby had a dream that Diana was with another woman. Not fully recovered, but well enough to return back to work, Abigail was greeted by her coworkers swarming her desk with a plethora of questions, greetings, and well-wishes. There were people who were truly happy to see her back. Diana was not one of them; she was not happy – she wanted back in. Upon seeing Abby's beautiful smile and her cheerful countenance, Diana wanted her back. Later that day, while at work, Diana texted Abby and asked if they could meet up and talk. Abby agreed to hear Diana out. Diana tried to talk a good game to persuade Abigail to get back with her. Abigail then posed a question to Diana that required her to answer truthfully about her behavior that she displayed while Abby was at her house trying to recover. Diana had advised Abigail that the reason why she was in and out during her time of recovery was because she was sleeping with another woman. Abby then let Diana in on the dream she had when she returned home to complete her recovery. Abby remained resolute on not reconciling with Diana. Diana was upset and walked away from Abigail unhappy.

℘

Abigail and Diana saw each other every day at work. Abigail was cordial with Diana, but nothing more than that. Diana still called and texted Abigail, which did nothing to Abby's resolve on staying apart from her. Preying on Abigail's kindness, knowing how helpful Abby was, Diana texted Abby that she was having car troubles and that she was in need of a ride home from the mechanic shop where she had taken her car to be fixed. Just as Diana knew she would, Abby came to Diana's rescue. While Abigail was dropping Diana off at home, Diana turned to Abigail and began to kiss her, professing her love and letting her know how the grass was not greener on the other side and that all she wanted was to be back with Abby. Diana begged and pleaded for Abigail to forgive her. Abigail fell for the okie doke and got back with Diana. That night, Abigail stayed with Diana. Diana was happy.

℘

After a while, things had been going well with Abby and Diana, so much so that Abby had decided to introduce Diana to her family. There was an annual memorial celebration for Abby's grandmother that was coming up, and she had decided on presenting Diana to her family at this event.

The time for the celebration weekend was upon them. With the car serviced, fully gassed up, AirBnB booked, Abby and Diana hit the road and headed to Abby's hometown to enjoy the family festivities. Abby and Diana made it into town, checked into their AirBnB, and got settled in. The next day, Abby and Diana headed on their way to

Grandmother's celebration. Upon arriving, Abby had introduced Diana to her family as her friend, but anyone with eyes or common sense could tell that they were, in fact, a couple. A good time was had by all. Abby and Diana received no discouraging remarks from her family at all. Diana was, in fact, welcomed with open arms. Abigail and Diana had partied pretty late into the evening with Abby's family before they had said their good nights and headed back to their AirBnB. On their last day in town, Abby and Diana went to the beach, where they enjoyed the water, the people, the food, and each other. While at the beach, Abby felt like doing something spontaneous, so she got Diana's name tattooed on her arm. The love Abby had for Diana was growing more and more with each passing day. Abigail and Diana returned home.

℘

A few months had passed since their trip to Abby's hometown. Abby had moved out of her aunt's house and into her own apartment. Abby invited a few of her friends from work over for a small housewarming party. A good time was had by all. At this time, Abby and Diana no longer worked together. Diana began working for a different company, but this time around it was Diana that was practically living with Abby, spending almost every night with her.

It was not long before Abby began to see a shift in Diana's behavior once again. Diana started going home after work and when she did come over to Abby's, she would say or do something that caused her and Abby to have a disagreement. When Diana arrived at Abby's the following night, Abby advised Diana that they should no longer be in a relationship.

Abigail said, "*I see you're falling back into the same old pattern again.*"

This time Diana agreed with Abby for she felt the same way. Diana advised Abby that she had in fact met someone at her new job and that she believed them to be in love. Abigail wished them well.

℘

Now separated from Diana, Abigail began to clear her mind. She began working out, hiking, eating right, watching sermons online, reading books, and even listening to worship music again. One day at work, in the break room, Abigail came across a woman named Valerie that worked in a different department. Valerie introduced Abigail to a whole different world, the world of entrepreneurship. Outside of work, Valerie took Abigail to business plan seminars, to meetings with millionaires, and even to her church on Sundays. Abigail was feeling renewed and focused on her future. Abigail knew that in order to move on from Diana, she had to block her. She completely blocked her on her phone and on social media platforms. Diana had no access to her whatsoever. Abigail clearly let it slip her mind that Diana knew her address because after 3 months without any correspondence Diana popped up at Abigail's doorstep yet again. Abigail was totally confused as to why Diana was standing before her. She was completely sure that she would never see Diana again after their last split. Abigail truly believed that this new woman that Diana was in love with would totally maintain her attention. Abigail was completely wrong. Diana came with a good sob story this time. The story she provided Abigail to get back in this time was that she had broken up with the woman she thought she was in love with, she lost her job, and she could no longer afford to live in her condo. Of course she felt secure in laying this story upon Abigail, the woman whom she was never in love with, but the woman who was always in love with her. Abigail, feeling confident and in a good headspace, Abby let Diana know that she could stay with her until she got back on her feet. It took Diana a couple of months to get everything squared away. As far as her condo was concerned and all her belongings placed into a storage unit, she was all moved in with Abigail. Abigail informed Diana from the gate that she was not willing to get back into a relationship with her, but that she was just extending a helping hand to Diana. Diana had agreed to a friendship. She even agreed to the living arrangements Abigail had set in place. Abigail had arranged for Diana to sleep in her second bedroom and not in the bed with her.

With this newfound friendship between Abigail and Diana, Diana introduced Abigail to her family via phone calls and sometimes via FaceTime. Diana's family took an instant liking to Abigail. Abigail felt a strong connection to Diana's older sister Melissa. Whenever Abby and Mel would talk, they would discuss the scriptures. Upon hearing Diana's conversations with her family, Abigail clearly understood why it took so long for Diana to introduce her to her family. Almost every conversation Diana had with multiple family members, they all were telling her the same thing, to repent of her sinful lifestyle. They all professed their love for Diana, but not her choice in living. From the valuable nuggets Abigail had acquired in the time spent with Valerie, Abigail became laser-focused on starting her own business. Abigail had advised Diana to do the same, but all Diana could focus on was getting back in Abigail's bed. Diana was trying her hardest to get back with Abby. She was in awe of this new woman Abby had grown into. Diana had secured a new position with another company. Feeling confident about having a job again, Diana and Abigail began doing things together, like going to the shooting range, movies, and sometimes they would even go out to dinner. To celebrate Diana's new position, Abigail and Diana went out to dinner at a well-known five-star restaurant. The food, the atmosphere was great; a good time was had. When Abby and Diana returned home, what happened next between the two seemed to be inevitable. Diana had made her way back into Abigail's bed. Abigail felt a different energy come over her after sleeping with Diana. Abigail stepped into her masculine energy. Abigail told Diana, "*We are not together. We are just having sex. That's it. That's all.*"

Abby also advised Diana *"Remain focused on getting back on your feet so you can move out and back on your own again."*

Diana really felt some type of way. Diana thought that once she slept with Abby that Abby was going to be a sucker for her version of love.

℘

Now, it was during this time that Abigail began to build a stronger sisterhood bond with Diana's older sister, Melissa. Melissa, an entrepreneur, already the president and CEO of her own company - was also a mighty woman of The Most High Yahuah. Abby and Mel had a lot to bond over. They bonded over business conversations, Biblical conversations, and even sometimes relationship conversations. Meanwhile, since things hadn't turned out with Abigail the way Diana had expected them to, she began to act a plum fool. She began coming home at 2 A.M. sometimes, not coming home at all. She would start arguments and even go as low as to tell Abby that her black (skin complexion) was not beautiful. Now that Abigail was back to Bible study and her headspace was clear, she could recognize the voice of her Abba Yahuah and she could *totally* recognize that the enemy/Satan was using Diana as a tool to try to break her. Abigail advised Diana that she had to leave and that she can go live wherever it was she was staying at all night. Through tears and pleas, Diana convinced Abigail that she had nowhere else she could live, and so Abby conceded and allowed Diana to stay.

℘

Over the next few months, Diana was fired and then hired from at least four different companies. Abby was coming to her wits end. It had gotten to the point that they argued consistently. They even found things to argue about in the grocery store. One morning, while Diana was at work, Abigail reached out to Mel.

Abby told Mel, "*You know what, I did this. I opened the door to the spirit of sexual perversion by watching lesbian pornography*".

Abby then went on to tell Mel about all that had transpired between her and Diana over the course of their relationship. She told her *everything*!

Mel told Abby, "*Repent, sis, repent and take communion.*"

As soon as Mel told Abby to repent, her heart went to 1 John 1:9 "*If we confess our sins, He is faithful and just to forgive us our sins, and to cleanse us from all unrighteousness.*"

Abigail and Mel prayed, cried, and thanked the Most High Yahuah for what he was about to do in Abigail's life. Abigail began to put a plan in motion. Abigail went online to apply for a job with a prominent company where she could work from home. Abigail also applied for a job with a prominent company on Diana's behalf. Abigail passed every test and assessment that was required prior to getting hired. The only thing Diana had to do was pass the drug screening and complete the job interview process. With the constant arguing, Abigail no longer felt comfortable in her own home. It was like she was living in a war zone, ducking and dodging landmines. Upon completion of the drug screening and the interview process, Diana was hired.

℘

With three paychecks saved, one morning when Diana left for work - Abigail packed up all Diana's belongings in the bins she brought them in, and placed them in the storage closet on the patio. When Diana got off work that evening, she returned home to Abigail's apartment to find the lock bolted and a note taped to the door for her to read. Diana was at a loss on what her next move should be. Diana called Mel, her mother, she even called the police. Mel completely understood Abby's actions. Diana's mother, Abby had to quote scripture, for the police she had to quote her lawful rights. Needless to say, Diana vacated the premises that night.

Once Abby had repented of her wicked ways, The Holy Spirit had told Abby to put that wicked spirit out of her apartment. Abby devised a plan to do just that, put that wicked spirit that was upon Diana out of her apartment. Abby knew she would need to get far away from Diana. She worked from home now, and she knew that she could take her job anywhere she went.

Abigail applied for an apartment about 1,200 miles away from Diana. She completed the application process. Afterwards, Abigail was approved for the new apartment.

Two months after Abigail put Diana out of her apartment, she packed up a U-Haul, and headed out of state, Abigail was on her way to a new place with no worries of Diana showing up on her doorstep ever again.

Summary/Conclusion Part 3:

- Abigail opened the door to sexual perversion by watching/consuming lesbian pornography. Abigail and Diana were broken. In this broken place a spirit of perversion influenced and clouded their perception on how they related to women.
- Abigail had the tendency to be motherly to Diana, in part since Abigail was told she could not have any children of her own. Abigail felt the need to nurture and coddle Diana.
- The Most High Yahuah allowed this experience to happen to Abigail. Abigail needed to gain an understanding of how that perverted spirit operates that is in control over the LGBTQ+ realm. How it looks, how it sounds, and its main objective: which is to get as many people as it can to be in rebellion to the commands of The Most High Yahuah.

- Abigail equates her experience of being in a relationship with a woman like eating from the tree of the knowledge of good and evil. Abigail tasted that The Most High Yahuah is good and she also tasted that rebelling against Him is evil. In the beginning the fruit tasted so sweet to Abigail, then after a few bites the fruit began to taste oh so bitter.
- Just when Abigail began to lose her identity in Yahuah, her Abba Yahuah showed up to remind her Who she was, and Whose she was.

Part 4:
The King and I

Headed to a new state with a renewed mind, Abigail was ready for a new season. Prior to Abigail moving to a new state, during the two months of her application process, The Most High Yahuah had begun to reveal to her who the so-called African American's true identity was. Abigail watched a three-part documentary called "***Reclaiming the Throne***" almost every day to gain an in-depth understanding of her true heritage/history. Watching this documentary caused Abigail to get back to studying the word of Yahuah more intently and consistently. One night before bed Abigail went to her usual streaming platform to pull up a movie to watch, in the feed of recommendations was a documentary called, "***Hebrew Israelites Debunked***." Abigail kept scrolling because she had thought that the platform's algorithm was making specific selections based on her previous history of watching "***Reclaiming the Throne.***" Once Abigail had scrolled past it she could hear the Ruach Ha'qodesh say, "*Watch it.*"

Being obedient to the Ruach Ha'qodesh, Abigail scrolled back to the documentary and pressed play. From the opening scene Abigail knew that this was going to be another revelation from The Most High Yahuah about us as a people. The eloquent speaker captured her full attention. Upon viewing this masterpiece of a story, Abigail saw clips of the orator standing at a pulpit teaching his congregation. Abigail thought, "*Wow this orator is a Pastor/Shepherd over a flock teaching/guiding them into truth.*"

Abigail was immediately drawn, for she was always in search of knowledge, wisdom, and truth. Abigail yearned to learn more from Pastor, so she sought out the platforms he taught lessons on. The main platform where she found him was Facebook - every Sunday, Wednesday, and Saturday. Abigail did not miss a chance to hear the orator speak. The Pastor also held an early morning Zoom Bible study on Saturdays. It started off with Abigail watching the Zoom meeting on Facebook, then one day an onlooker asked the question of how they could be a part of the actual zoom meeting. The Zoom meeting ID and password were given. Abigail wrote it down and the following Shabbat, Abigail became an official member of the pastor's Shabbat Zoom Bible study.

℘

Abigail had driven 1,200 miles and she had finally arrived at her new apartment with a U-Haul full of her furniture and belongings. Abigail had no idea how she was going to get all her stuff inside the apartment. Abigail just kept saying to herself that her Abba Yahuah will have a ram in the bush. Abigail began to unload what she could carry from the U-Haul. As Abigail came out of her apartment to get what she could, the new upstairs neighbor noticed Abigail's solo mission in unloading the U-Haul. Her neighbor asked, "*You got somebody to help you get that stuff?*"

Abigail replied, "*I do not.*" The neighbor grabbed his nephew and they began to unload all the heavy items from the U-Haul into Abigail's apartment. Abigail praised Yahuah for His provision. With the U-Haul now empty and the apartment filled with all of Abigail's furniture and belongings, Abigail paid her new neighbors $50 each and thanked them profusely for helping her out in her time of need.

Abigail, all settled and getting acclimated to the new state in her new apartment, did not miss a beat in attending Shabbat Zoom Bible study on Saturday mornings. Three months into being a part of the Zoom meeting, watching and listening to Pastor teach on Wednesday nights and twice on Sunday mornings, Abigail perceived that her thoughts and beliefs were being renewed/transformed. Mel had recommended Abigail read a new Bible, the Cepher Bible, a Bible that included the Apocrypha as well as the Hebrew Lexicon so she could learn how to read and write in Hebrew. Abigail's Abba Yahuah was revealing His word to her in ways she had never seen before. Oh, she had read the Bible before, but now the eyes of her understanding had been opened. The truth of her Abba Yahuah, Abigail was beginning to grasp. One Wednesday night Bible study, Abigail was not present online due to a change in her shift at work, when she was DM'd (directly messaged) by one of the members of Pastor's Zoom meeting/church inquiring of her well-being as he had grown accustomed to her being in attendance. The King that reached out to Abigail, Michael, was one of the members of the flock that followed Pastor so intently that he called Pastor "Dad." Michael and Pastor were so awesome with the word together that Abigail called them "*the dynamic duo*." Abigail replied back to Michael and let him know why she had not attended Wednesday night's Bible study. Michael had informed Abigail of his intentions of getting to know her better. Abigail had never seen

Michael's face; a she had grown accustomed to selecting her partners based off of their outward appearance (i.e...looks). Abigail had a talk with her Abba. She could hear her Abba Yahuah say, "*Would you prefer a man that looks good or a man that knows and follows me*?"

Abigail chose the latter, and without seeing Michael's face, she agreed to them getting to know one another better. The next day, Michael and Abigail made confessions to one another of their past relationship experiences and what perversions The Most High Yahuah had delivered them both from. Once Michael perceived how gracious, kind, and understanding Abigail was, he was ready to reveal himself to her on a video chat. "*You ready to see my face now,*" he asked. Abigail certainly was.

King Michael called Abigail through Facebook Messenger. When King Michael's face appeared on her screen, Abigail laughed. She immediately thought her Abba has a sense of humor. King Michael was extremely handsome. A couple of days went by and King Michael and Abigail talked every chance they could throughout the day, on into the night. One night while they were talking, King Michael had advised Abigail that he did not like women that smoked. Meanwhile, Abigail had just purchased her weekly ounce of marijuana. Abigail said nothing to King Michael right away about her habit. About an eighth into her ounce, Abigail made King Michael aware of her habit. King Michael prayed for her and with her immediately. With King Michael on video chat, Abigail went to grab what was left of her sack, proceeded to the restroom, and flushed the remains down the toilet. Abigail was amazed at what she had just done. Abigail knew that she wanted to be with King Michael, so her vice had to go. Abigail perceived that King Michael made her desire to be a better woman. The next day, King Michael asked Abigail to marry him. Actually, he stated, "*Oh, you are my wife. I'm gonna marry you.*" Abigail agreed. She was enamored.

A few more weeks went by when King Michael and Abigail put into motion plans to see each other in person. Abigail put in the days off at work, packed up a few items in her suitcase, and headed to the rental car company, where she was turned away. Abigail then went online and booked a flight; she was determined to see her love. Abigail and King Michael were extremely excited to see one another, to touch, kiss, embrace. They had decided it was time. Abigail could feel the butterflies in her belly. Assuming all preparations were complete, Abigail began to reach out to the ride share company to escort her to the airport, when in that moment the Ruach Ha'qodesh told her to check her flight information. Abigail had booked the flight for the right city, wrong state. Abigail informed King Michael of all the stumbling blocks that were popping up when it came to them meeting in person. King Michael and Abigail had determined that the Most High Yahuah was not in agreement with what they had planned. Abigail felt kind of disappointed. She was absolutely ready to touch, feel, kiss, embrace this prize of a king that the Most High Yahuah had led her to.

Abigail began to unpack her suitcase. She could hear the Ruach Ha'qodesh ask her, "*Where's your divorce papers*?" Abigail began looking through her documents and realized that she had never completed the divorce process from Gabriel. Later that evening, when King Michael called Abigail, she advised him about what she had discovered in regard to her divorce, and that she was in fact still a married woman. King Michael and Abigail immediately understood why their meeting was obstructed. The Most High Yahuah, saved them from breaking Torah by committing adultery. In both of their minds, they had already determined that sex was going to be had once Abigail arrived in King Michael's town. Waiting until after marriage was the last thing on their minds. Just collect $200 and pass GO!!! King Michael and Abigail praised

Yahuah for his divine protection. The following weeks, Abigail gathered all the information she needed to proceed forward with divorcing Gabriel and executed. Abigail made multiple trips to the courthouse, all while continuing to FaceTime with King Michael.

With her continued attendance at the Zoom Bible Studies on Saturday mornings, learning and gleaning from Pastors' lessons on Sunday morning, King Michael had begun to conduct Bible studies with Abigail, just the two of them, their own little family Bible study. Before Abigail knew it, five months had gone by, and she had her divorce decree in hand. Abigail walked out of that courthouse feeling so free. King Michael and Abigail expeditiously planned another trip for Abigail to come visit him in his hometown. King Michael and Abigail had now officially been together for eight months. King Michael had organized for their marriage ceremony to take place as well while Abigail was in town. This time, the flight was arranged for the correct city and state. King Michael booked the rental car and hotel stay. All was well. Two weeks after Abigail had received her divorce decree, she was standing in the airport of King Michael's hometown awaiting his arrival (her flight even landed early.) :)

She saw him. There he was, King Michael, approaching Abigail. Looking good, clean-shaven, beard lined up ever so neat, with the bouquet of roses and calla lilies in hand, (Abigail's favorites) and a big smile on his face. When King Michael reached Abigail, he smelled oh-so-amazing, wearing a scent called "*I Am King*." They instantly embraced and kissed one another for what seemed to be forever. Bouquet in one hand and King Michael's hand in the other, Abigail and King Michael exited the airport overjoyed to finally be in one another's presence. Abigail almost felt giddy, like she was young again. It was truly satisfying being in the presence of a real man, a mighty man of Yahuah. King Michael and Abigail headed to their hotel where they would get prepared for their covenant ceremony. This ceremony was very private. It would include King Michael, Abigail, Pastor, and his First Lady/Wife. The groom, the bride, two witnesses and The Most High Yahuah. The ceremony took place at Pastor's beautiful home where it felt peaceful and tranquil. King Michael and Abigail entered Pastor's home. Prior to the inception of the ceremony, they all greeted one another with hugs and pleasantries. The ceremony took place without any mishaps. King Michael and Abigail declared their vows to one another that they had written. Rings were exchanged. The groom kissed his bride. Their witnesses signed their vows. King Michael and Abigail were now in an eternal covenant with one another.

Pastor and First Lady fed them, then sent them on their way to consummate their marriage. On the ride back to their hotel, Abigail had butterflies in her stomach. This was the first time she had done things in decency and in order. King

Michael was a real man, a man's man, a mighty man of Yahuah, a man Abigail prayed for, now her King, her Husband, Her Lord. Abigail was absolutely looking forward to becoming one with King Michael.

℘

For the next four days, King Michael showed Abigail around his town, and at night, they consummated repeatedly. Abigail was extremely pleased with the wonderful man her Abba Yahuah had led her to. King Michael and Abigail could not get enough of each other. On the night before Abigail was to return home, she shared with King Michael a list that she had written up seven years prior to meeting him. The list was comprised of all the attributes she desired in a husband, and out of the 23 attributes listed, King Michael had 18. King Michael was definitely Abigail's answered prayers. Abigail was enamored once again.

The following morning, King Michael and Abigail checked out of their hotel, had some breakfast, then headed to the airport. The drive felt as though they were walking the green mile. King Michael was driving so slowly that he almost caused Abigail to miss her flight. King Michael and Abigail quickly hugged and kissed and said, "*Until we see each other again, (no goodbyes).*"

Abigail aboard the plane, King Michael in the car, watching the plane leave the runway. Tears were shed. Once Abigail reached her apartment, she called King Michael to let him know she had a safe trip home. King Michael had informed Abigail that when her plane had taken off, he felt as though a piece of him had been taken away. Abigail was enamored. The next few days consisted of King Michael on the hunt for an apartment big enough for him and his new bride to start a new life together. Three weeks after they were married, Abigail had all her belongings packed and ready to go. King Michael paid for movers to load her furniture and belongings into the U-Haul. Abigail was on the road again, headed to be with her new husband.

King Michael called Abigail every 30 minutes to get an update on her location and her well-being. This drive took a toll on Abigail. One state outside of her new hometown, and it was like the bottom had fallen out of the sky. It was pouring down raining. King Michael and Abigail prayed to Abba Yahuah for traveling mercies and Abigail pushed through to get to her King. Abigail reached her new hometown safely. She arrived at their new apartment where King Michael was waiting for her. They embraced and kissed each other even longer than they had at their first meeting in the airport. That night, King Michael took Abigail to have dinner at one of his favorite restaurants nearby where the food was amazing. King Michael recommended his favorite dish, which was chicken alfredo with sweet garlic bread. It was delicious. Upon returning home, King Michael and Abigail had had a long day. The only items they unloaded from the U-Haul that night were their mattress, bedding, washcloths and towels, and TV. King Michael made love to his new bride, then they fell asleep, as they wrapped up in each other's arms together.

℘

With the U-Haul unloaded and returned, King Michael and Abigail began to build a life together. They began learning one another better, learning each other's likes and dislikes as far as how a house should be kept/run. They were also learning things that they both liked to do to pass the time on their days off from work, like watching movies, hanging with family, racing R.C cars or just a good home cooked meal and chilling with each other was pleasant too. King Michael had incorporated their family Bible study every night before they went to bed. Abigail became a member of the church. She began to build bonds and sisterhoods with a couple of the sisters at the church. The more King Michael and Abigail studied the word of Yahuah and applied it to their lives; the more they could see that the Most High Yahuah was creating in them a clean heart and an upright spirit. They both were at peace. The Most High Yahuah had led them to still waters.

Summary/Conclusion Part 4:

- Abigail began to listen to The Ruach within. Abigail began to be obedient to The Ruach Ha'qodesh.
- Abigail remembered who The Most High Yahuah has been to her throughout her entire life. A Keeper, Provider, her Protector, her Abba.
- Abigail was drawn to the truth. Abigail heard the voice of her Shepherd and followed him. The Most High Yahuah led Abigail to a Shepherd that followed Him, that knew Him.
- Abigail was processed and prepared for King Michael through the lessons she learned from life's experiences. Abigail was purposed for King Michael by her Abba Yahuah. Abigail was willing to make whatever changes were necessary for her to be with King Michael.

- Abigail's experiences allowed her to understand King Michael and how to love him properly (respect/honor). Abigail knew that her marriage to King Michael was Yahuah ordained.

No L's Just Lessons

No losses - just extracted lessons out of every life experience.

*(Changing our mindset from <u>Victim</u> to **Victor**)*

- Abigail experienced no loss in being abandoned by her human father, for she learned that she had the best Father a girl could ask for, Abba Yahuah (perfect in every way).

- Abigail experienced no loss in not having children with Gabriel, for she learned to have faith in her Abba Yahuah's timing. Abigail learned the perfection of patience.

- Abigail experienced no loss in divorcing Gabriel, for she learned that her Abba Yahuwah requires her to be equally yoked with her spouse.

- Abigail experienced no loss when she had to live in hotels and a car, for she learned that her Abba

Yahuah always makes a way out of no way, that her Abba Yahuah is a provider.

- Abigail experienced no loss when a brother in Ha'mashiach took what she did not freely give, for she learned to no longer be naive and to discern the correct/best environments/situations to place herself in.

- Abigail experienced no loss when Grandmother was called home to be with The Most High Yahuah, for she learned that her Abba Yahuah always supplied her with a guardian angel.

- Abigail experienced no loss when Gabriel chose to be with another woman, for she learned that her Abba Yahuah required her to be with someone that treated her better than Gabriel had. Abigail experienced no loss when Gabriel spoke death to her womb, for she learned that her Abba Yahuah would send her to a Mighty man of Yahuah that would speak life to her womb.

- Abigail experienced no loss by being in a relationship with Diana, nor breaking it off with Diana, for she learned through meeting Diana her Abba Yahuah guided her to the realest, most genuine sisterhood she has ever experienced in her entire lifetime through Melissa/Mel. Abigail experienced no loss by her breakup with Diana for she learned that her Abba Yahuah could have given her over to a reprobate mind.

Final Thoughts:

I was anointed to speak life into others. The Most High Yahuah has given/equipped/gifted me to understand words and how to use them properly. I have been anointed to use words to caress, uplift, encourage, edify, motivate, and inspire my beautiful sisters in Ha'mashiach spiritually. The enemy does not know your future, nor your calling. He studies your talents and your gifts, and what he does is assign certain demonic spirits to attach themselves to you, to silence or diminish and block those gifts and talents. The enemy knows that if you tap into the Ruach Ha'qodesh, that your gifts and your talents will now have power behind them, propelling them, uplifting them to the light for all men and women to see. Once we tap into our anointing, our authority, we become a beacon of light for all men and women to see, and all the glory goes to The Most High Yahuah when people begin to ask questions on what's got you glowing. Keep sight of what's real. Do not be deceived by the enemy. Know when thoughts are of the Ruach Ha'qodesh and when they are of a wicked spirit. We must use discernment. We must rebuke and renounce every wicked spirit once we recognize it. In the mighty name of Yahusha Ha'Mashiach.

We must stay in the word of Yahuah daily in order to know the voice of Yahuah. The flesh is weak, but the Ruach is willing to do the will of the Most High Yahuah. So many of US are searching to find OURSELVES or don't know who WE are because WE have too many spirits coming and going, leaving US confused. The Most High Yahuah did not give us a spirit of confusion, but one of power, love, and a sound mind. I found my identity when I found Yahusha Ha'Mashiach.

There is peace in Yahusha Ha'Mashiach. There is joy, and there is clarity. Once peace is obtained, you have joy, and once you have the two, you now have clarity of the mind. Know what is good and what is Holy. We must be spirit-led and spirit-fed to have a clear head. Without clarity, we don't learn, we don't grow. Without the infilling of the Ruach Ha'qodesh, we cannot be transformed, nor can our minds be renewed. We must allow the Ruach Ha'qodesh to have His perfect way. We must surrender to Him. We must remember that we are spiritual beings having a human experience. Therefore, we must focus on the Ruach and rebuke the desires of our flesh. We must prove to the Most High Yahuah that we are not in a relationship with Him just for show. We cannot be fruitful if we are flighty. We cannot be fruitful if we are not faithful. Being in a relationship with the Most High Yahuah is an auspicious experience. It can be humbling at times. It can be liberating. It can be downright revelatory. Times may get tough, but the reward we shall reap is worth fighting for. We must endure.

The Word of the Most High Yahuah is meant for three things: to reveal Yahuah's ways and His purpose, to impart

Yahuah's wisdom and strength, to correct so that we walk in Yahuah's truth and to be made righteous. Those not following the ways of the Most High Yahuah, are under a spell of the dark world. Anyone that does not give Yahuah the glory is under a spell of the dark world. Anyone that does not worship nor praise the Almighty Yahuah, is under a spell of the dark world. All these things (obedience, glory, worship, and praise) are done in deed, not with just lip service. Children of the Most High Yahuah the Bride of Yahusha are doers of Yahuah's word, not just hearers. We cannot serve two masters. We will love the one and hate the other. We cannot serve the Most High Yahuah, and our flesh. Believe it, receive it, and you can achieve it. May the Most High Yahuah bless the readers of this testimony. May He open up the eyes of your understanding. In the mighty name of Yahusha Ha'Mashiach, Hallelu Yah.

About the Author

Latisha Hanger, born in Pasadena California, is a wife, daughter, sister, and aunt with a heart of a servant. She has a strong desire to help others, especially her sisters in Mashiach to be in alignment with the will of The Most High Yahuah.

As wife to a mighty man of Yah, it is her hope that what she has gleaned from her Abba Yahuah and her Husband Lord may be passed on to Yah's people.

The experiences that Latisha has written, The Most High Yah allowed them so that this testimony might save those that receive it.

Zoë Life Publishing

Zoë Life Publishing is a publishing imprint that releases titles committed to offering encouragement and that are life transforming. We desire for our titles to impact readers in a way that is beyond entertainment; a way that will bring healing, restoration, or even productivity to one's life. Our catalogue includes now children's titles, notebooks, and journals.

Scan the QR code below to visit our website today for more information.

www.ingramcontent.com/pod-product-compliance
Lightning Source LLC
LaVergne TN
LVHW010935110826
845149LV00013B/2604

* 9 7 9 8 9 9 2 7 3 6 0 3 8 *